A book by Vibhuti Purohit

DIVE IN UX

an overall guide to understand User Experience

Design an Experience | Design a Living

First Published in February 2023

ISBN: 978-93-5668-533-8

BLUEROSE PUBLISHERS
www.BlueRoseONE.com
info@bluerosepublishers.com
+91 8882 898 898

Cover Design:
Vibhuti Purohit

Cover Image Credit:
https://mcc.gse.harvard.edu/whats-new/barbados-today-empathetic-communication-a-viable-tool-to-avoid-conflicts

Typographic Design:
Pooja Sharma

Distributed by: BlueRose, Amazon, Flipkart

Acknowledgement

Writing this book was a significant duty that I put on myself. The goal was no to create a commercial commodity in academia, but to be able to give something valuable to those who want to work in the design profession. It took a lot of time, patience, and the support of people who kept me encouraged throughout the process to accomplish this task.

First and foremost, I'd like to thank my parents, Sanju and Manju, as well as my brother Somya, who have always supported my professional decisions, from choosing to be a designer rather than an engineer to taking on the responsibility of publishing a solo book.

I'd like to thank my UX mentors, Mr. Ashvesh and Mr. Rakesh, for shaping me into the professional person I am today. Their sincere instructions have made me a keen and eager learner of the subject.

I also want to thank my friends Shagun and Silvi, who were there living with me and encouraging me to buckle up, and Dipanshu, who I always looked forward to talking to, when I felt hopeless and thought about giving up at times.

They have been there to encourage me throughout the process whenever I have felt nervous about juggling between my career, family, and other work.

Finally, I'd like to thank myself for having faith in my ability to be an independent au0thor and for maintaining a sense of balance in all aspects of my life.

Preface

People generally ask me how to go into user experience, either through my past college references, any friends or family, or through social media platforms. In addition to having expertise in the field, I am a qualified User Experience designer with a Master's in design (specializing in UX design). Any aspiring enthusiast who is willing to break into this field can get a deep insight in this book.

Therefore, you must advance your skill gradually and efficiently in order to gain a thorough understanding of what User Experience is. I believe that your intense interest in the subject will help you establish a fruitful career as a UX specialist. The only things that can lead you to your career goal, just like my journey did for me, are your curiosity and desire to learn more.

I am not an experienced book author, but I published this book for all of my readers because I am passionate about this subject and want to share my knowledge in a way that even a novice can understand UX. Even a single life with this book would be the greatest success and happiness as a new author.

To be completely honest, the original plan was to write a book that would be an expanded version of my "Alcohol Addiction" master's thesis. Then, I made the decision to write about my motivation for concentrating on the "Alcohol Addiction" problem rather than the subject itself.

Although there are many places to learn about UX, this book focuses on how to understand and dive deep into the topic. This book presents all of the subjects in the same way that I personally prefer to acquire and impart knowledge. There will be a greater understanding of User Experience among all of my readers. In addition, the format of this book ensures that readers will benefit from an efficient learning process in addition to learning about user experience.

About the Author

This is the debut book by Indian author Vibhuti Purohit, who transitioned from writing content to sustain her monthly expenses while in college to becoming a trained User Experience Designer. She had a deep interest in writing and worked as a freelance content writer for her pocket money. When she was a high school student, she discovered a hidden passion for writing and composed a little poem recalling her school time memories.

Being a Master's degree holder and an industrial professional, she considered combining her writing passion and professional experience to create this book. In her belief, "Learning without imparting knowledge would be worthless."

About the Book

This book was conceptualized and written at the same time.

The idea of producing a book early in her career came to the author since she is a working professional and a lifelong learner of user experience and she believes that if the book was written concurrently with being a working professional, it might incorporate knowledge from an industrial perspective as well.

Hence, the book contains all the essential knowledge required to begin a career in user experience. Because the book emphasizes learning more than just the "Jargons taught with jargons," readers will find it easier to adapt to the User Experience perspective with all aspects.

Contents

Chapter-1

User Experience Design

Once upon a time, there was an engineer who worked for a gadget manufacturer on product development. He was in the middle of a process in which the team was considering the demands and positioning of the product in the market from the customer's perspective. A concept stuck in his thoughts, prompting him to consider what he had been doing and why he had been doing so. He kept thinking for a long time because he wanted to know why he and everyone else had been thinking about all these considerations. He eventually narrowed down the explanations and established a word that encompassed all his inquiries. You've probably guessed the engineer's name by now. If not, you may question, "Who is the Father of User Experience or UX?" He's the one we've been talking about, the one who coined the term **'User Experience', Don Norman.**

'As he defined and the title itself implies, the involvement of two key aspects in every step of bringing a problem to a conclusion. The two factors are:

User + Experience

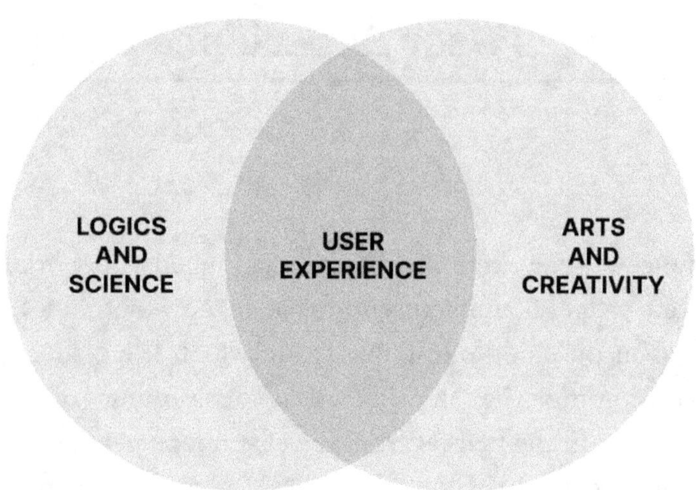

User refers to the individual for whom the conclusion is being developed, and whose needs and demands form the foundation of any product. A user is a person who uses something, and the term is usually always used to refer to what they are using. As a result, they're regarded as the foundation of any product (digital or Physical). Product development is like democracy

for the user, of the user, and by the user

as anyone or everyone has been a user at one time or another.

The entire process of assessing the user's wants and desires for the development of any product revolves around one important factor: how the user will react to what they have in their hands or how they will feel when engaged in a process or using a physical product. This is the definition of the term "experience," and it is from this definition that the term "User Experience" was coined. This is when the method was first acknowledged, even though it had been used for a long time.

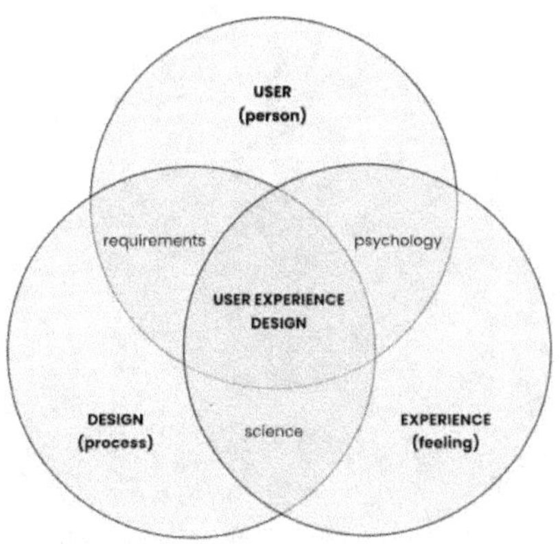

User Experience Design is a branch of design that considers a variety of aspects to build everything around you be it tangible or virtual. As shown in the diagram above,

a user is a person who has a feeling during an experience and for whom the design process is carried out to meet the requirements that he must have had, considering his psychology and the science/technology that is best suited. The primary base of any product is how the user interacts with it. There isn't much of a difference between a physical and a digital product in terms of user experience. Let's take a closer look at how the concept of User Experience plays a role in both cases in the next chapter.

Chapter-2

Day to Day User Experience: Physical and Digital

We depend entirely on the products, services, and a wide range of facilities that technology and growth have made accessible to us to survive in today's world. We should be grateful for the innovations and services we have today, yet we eventually manage to find flaws and drawbacks in each of them. We often experience discomfort and frustration when our comfort and luxury are even slightly compromised if things don't turn out the way we had expected.

We come into contact with various things from the moment we wake up until we go to bed, including toothbrushes, toothpaste, coke bottles, vehicles, refrigerators, television screens, air conditioners, dryers, microwaves, etc. Each product can be improved so that it will benefit the user. Because we have adapted to utilizing them and are used to them, we may not feel a need for an upgrade in every routine product. But as a user experience designer, I have seen how many of the goods and services we use on a regular basis might improve from a UX design perspective.

The emotional interaction that users have with a company's website, goods, services, apps, or other online communications is known as the user experience. I firmly believe that UX design has a far wider scope than what some people may think, who may limit it to websites, mobile applications, or any other digital media. I strongly think that better user experience design must be included in everything we use on a regular basis. To eliminate or at least reduce users' pain points, the user experience for everyone and everything should be improved.

UX for Physical Products

1. **Visual Experience-** Apple is a great example in and of itself, having popularised user experience design. A low LED level appears when a user puts a MacBook on the charge to show the charging status. A tiny LED that changes color depending on the charge level is located at the end of the charger that connects to the laptop. It changes color from red to green after charging is complete. As a result, the user can tell how much is being charged without even looking. The magnet in the charging port also makes it simpler to

locate the laptop's charging socket without having to seek it.

2. **Tangible experience-** The most common question asked while looking for new audio equipment is whether to get wired or wireless earbuds. How the experience of consumers has influenced the transition from a pair of wired earphones to a pair of wireless earbuds is an excellent example of UX in physical products.

3. **Generic Experience**- When compared to today, the majority of processes that required a lot of time before are now completed online. To improve the customer experience, this was done. This explains why improving the user or customer experience has always been the foundation of any user or customer journey while undergoing any process or product usage while engaging with any procedure or product.

"Observe the user without interfering with their interactions with the product or any procedures they find uncomfortable."

UX for Digital Products

In physical products, user experience refers to how a person feels when interacting with a particular product. It includes a range of feelings including emotional impact, mental model, and physical interaction. Everything that influences a user's interaction with a digital product is referred to as UX in the realm of digital design. When evaluating their experiences with a product, consumers frequently consider the following factors:

Value: Does this product offer me any benefit?

Function: Does this item really work?

Usability: Is it user-friendly?

Overall perception: Is it comfortable to use?

For instance, the majority of the growing generation uses the app to order meals on a regular basis, making Swiggy a household name in the Indian app market, particularly in the urban or semi urban areas.

Swiggy has seized on one of the most important needs—quenching hunger—with an intuitive design. Swiggy's main screen is noticeably cleaner than that of many of its rivals, and the placement of the ads doesn't appear out of place and fits in seamlessly with the other components. In addition to its attractive visuals, the app is so user-friendly that customers choose to place their orders using the app from the comfort of their homes and pay a small premium over doing so personally. Thus, we are aware that people would rather spend more money on a better and a good experience.

A satisfying user experience enables users to interact with a service or product. When customers are happy with our service, they are inclined to recommend it to others. This implies a rise in new users while retaining current ones. Focusing on the user, getting to know the user, and giving them a service they can use and a solution they can use are the objectives of good user experience. In other words, when a product's experience is intangible and the product seems seamless, the user experience is good.

As shown in the image below, we can clearly observe and infer that the second screen is what appears to be a good experience, whereas the first screen requires more effort to interpret than the second.

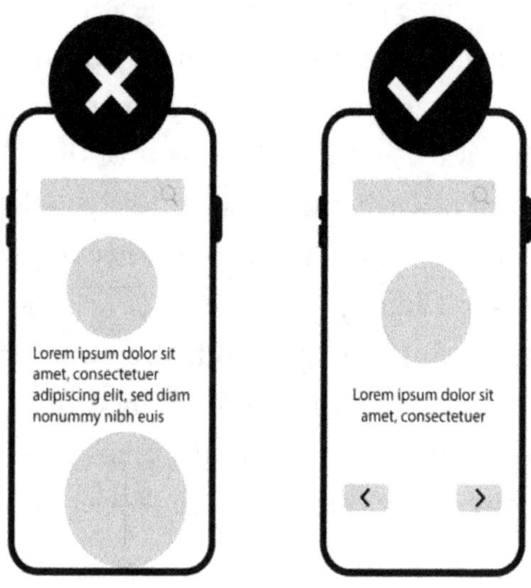

Chapter-3

UX Perspective

User experience is a process that we encounter in practically all aspects and contexts of daily life. We should all be comfortable and have the best experiences possible is what we as individuals expect in all we go through. Consequently, as aspiring user experience designers, we should be aware of all the areas where we may apply and broaden our thought process to produce any new experience or enhance any existing one. Each scenario is built around a particular objective that must be accomplished. The user experience can be created in a series of steps or a set of products that go toward reaching the desired outcome based on the results of the UX research.

UX in Marketing- The goal of marketing is to attract the attention of potential customers or clients in your goods and services. Herein lies the fact that we take into account the brand's target consumers or audiences while doing anything related to brand marketing. Everything we design, from social media graphics to television commercials, is done with an eye on what the public wants to see and how they want to be drawn to a product through various marketing techniques.

UX in Furniture Design- Furnitures' UX design is built on an understanding of the users, the environment, and their experiences. For instance, UX design considers the ergonomics of the brain while building technology, just like chairs are made with the support of the human body in mind. When creating seats, take into account the resources at your disposal and what you can make of them. Similar to this, the business and technological components of the product must be considered during UX design. Ergonomic furniture refers to things that have been developed with comfort, functionality, and human body mobility in mind. This style of furniture is becoming increasingly popular in contemporary office design ideas.

UX in Shopping Malls- A food court is something that practically every shopping mall in the world has. A food court is the section of the mall where all of the delicious cuisines are accessible. Because all of that walking and shopping might burn a lot of calories, the mall owners make sure you get your energy back and then some. Food courts are typically located on the top floor of shopping malls around the world. This is due to a variety of things, including people's psychology, experiences, and expectations. It is natural for humans to be distracted by the aroma of a delicious meal. If, for example, a food court is put on the ground floor, it may discourage customers from exploring the rest of the mall. Aside from that, because we've discovered that people prefer spending time at food courts, malls purposefully place them at the top. People may feel tempted to browse the shops on the lower floors and shop on their way to the food court even if they have no intention of purchasing anything.

UX in Filmmaking- A movie is either doing really well or it's a box office flop, as we've always heard. What gets more attention are the reviews that we read after each movie comes out. Throughout this, a recurring pattern has been noticed: the target audiences for which the films were created determine whether they are super hits or super flops, and they also influence the reviews. Therefore, in a sense, we can say that the experience of the viewers is the key factor that goes into the production of a movie. A movie is classified as a mega hit, a typical hit, or a failure movie depending on whether audience' experiences in that particular film are consistent with what they anticipate.

UX in QSR (Quick Service Restaurant)- A quick service restaurant (QSR) is an eatery that serves certain cuisine items that need little to no preparation and are delivered quickly. Quick service restaurants, often known as QSRs, typically specialize in fast food items over a small menu because they can be prepared with the least amount of variance in the least amount of time.

QSR restaurants are renowned for having standardized, flexible, and effective processes that enable them to shorten the lead times needed to complete orders while maintaining the level of quality that consumers expect. Since this is what most customers want, QSRs have evolved into a trend that the majority of businessmen consider opening rather than full-fledged restaurants or hotels. Nowadays, people expect their meals to be delivered quickly, which is why QSRs have been set up.

UX in Travel Planning- In the past, making travel arrangements usually involved going to a travel agent. You might obtain advice from travel agencies on where to go, how to get there, and which hotel to stay at. Today's technology makes it simple to find hotels, book flights, and organise activities with just the click of a mouse. With the Internet, you may act as your own travel agent, so there's no need to schedule an appointment.

You may even make reservations in advance for restaurants and purchase ready-to-pick-up tickets for amusement parks or concerts so that you can pick them up when you get there. This evolution was made possible by advances in technology and, most importantly, human experience.

We can relate our core UX to anything or everything now that we are aware of the various perspectives on user experience and how everything is created or designed in accordance with the experience expectations of the users, audience, or viewers. As a result, we will be able to make significant changes to our surroundings.

Chapter-4

Domains: UX is Everywhere

UX is everywhere, so what did I mean when I said that?

Is it any place we go, anything we see, or any industry or sector that comes to mind?

Yes, you have approached it right. Everywhere, IT IS. The idea that everything should be done comfortably, resulting in an improved "Experience," is evidence that UX is everywhere.

So let's take a closer look at some of the key areas where UX is crucial to the design and development of the overall process. Healthcare, Fintech, Ed-tech, E-commerce, Gaming, and E-governance are just a few of the sectors that will be briefly explored to demonstrate the idea that UX is present everywhere.

UX in Healthcare Industry- Due to recent technological breakthroughs, the Indian healthcare industry has undergone a rapid shift. Even while the quality of healthcare services may have improved, both the expense and complexity have significantly increased. UX was brought in to collaborate and improve the healthcare service keeping the users/customers in mind to swoop in and address these problems.

Regarding the improved experience, there are yet again two viewpoints to consider: Digital products as well as physical products and processes.

Healthcare in digital products

'Take it easy, PharmEasy'... You surely have heard this phrase in TV commercials or Digital advertisements. This is a healthcare service-providing platform, so let's examine and analyze this healthcare application briefly.

Many applications in the market cater to various healthcare needs, including the delivery of medications, laboratory tests, doctor consultations, etc. PharmEasy was launched in the market to create a single platform that addresses 4 key healthcare requirements and improves user experience.

Healthcare in physical products/processes

1. Physical product- The user experience has an impact on how physical products evolve in the healthcare industry. You'll understand what I mean when I say that this product altered through time, still

offering the same function but evolving in terms of utility and physical design.

Here is an example of how a conventional sphygmomanometer, which was previously mercury-based, then aneroid, and finally digital, has been modified to emphasize the ease and experience of its users (here, doctors). The only way to improve the device was purely based on making it easier to grasp the meter readings, making it more efficient and portable simultaneously.

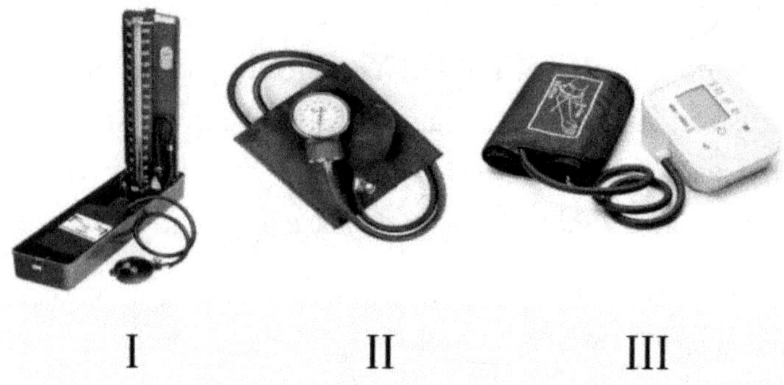

2. Physical process- Think about the procedure of waiting in line at a diagnostic lab for your turn to have your blood or urine sample collected. Following that, there were a couple of days waiting for the reports and a few days waiting to pick up your reports from the lab. Agh!!! It was a chaotic process, and according to those reports, it was almost late to begin the medication.

We then have got to go through a similar service provision process that is completely comfortable. Call, get your samples collected the same day, and the next day you'll have your reports by email, WhatsApp, etc. What a relief! This is where USER EXPERIENCE played a role in improving our lives by taking into account and upgrading USER EXPERIENCE.

UX in Fin-tech Industry- Fin-tech, a significant financial and technological collaboration, was made possible by the combination of traditional financial processes and technological innovation. In addition to providing more ease, this has helped many people save time and effort.

In terms of improved experience, there are two perspectives to consider: digital products as well as physical products and processes.

Fin-tech in digital products

Sharing expenses with buddies is never easy, especially when making online payments. By creating a payment plugin that can be included in any payment gateway or online payment system, a Fintech brand called "Payment Courier" set out to end this misery.

The user must be aware of the two payment choices available on the merchant's website—Direct Payment and Split Payment. For the user to select the best way for them, we wanted to inform them with quick text and tooltips. Following setup, we create a special, encrypted link that the Buyer must send to each Payer (s). Every participant can track the status of each payment with the provided link, which links them all to the same Payment Page.

Fin-tech in physical products/processes

1. Physical product- In addition to this, you've probably seen a gadget in manu offline stores with an online payment option that reads "You've received 'X' Rupees in your paytm" or "Paytm par 'X' Rupaye praapt huye." This device was developed in light of the fact that more customers are making in-person purchases online, making it challenging for the store owner to keep track of all the transactions in real time.

2. Physical process- In the banking industry, the Know Your Customer (KYC) process includes biometric verification in addition to ID card and face

verification as well as document and utility bill verification. In the past, individuals had to visit banks on their own, along with all the required documentation. The user/customer experience has since evolved, and the implementation of Video KYC has not only catered to their comfort but also sped up the service provision.

UX in Ed-Tech Industry- A smart user experience (UX) designer in education technology knows how to translate quality education and learning science into a digital learning tool. EdTech products must aid in effective learning, and UX designers have a specific responsibility in designing the elements that make learning easier. Your EdTech solution will be better, more useful, and more appealing to educators if you include research from learning science into the UX process. Additionally, it implies that you aren't following the newest EdTech trends. You're creating a product that is user-centric and based on research that is effective.

Ed-tech in digital products

Consider yourself in a crowded classroom as the instructor explains an important topic. Everyone else seems to be following along with the teacher's explanations by nodding their heads in approval, but you are unable to understand a single word of what is being said in class. A student's life has at least one instance of this type of circumstance. Since everyone learns at a different rate, the teacher cannot individually tutor every student in the class. This was the problem that bothered Raveendran Byju and gave rise to the app and wider business ecosystem developed as BYJU.

Ed-tech in physical products/processes

1.   Physical product- The black boards or white boards we have used since the start of our own educational journey are the first thing that comes to mind when we discuss education, schools, classrooms, etc. Observing today's classrooms, we can see that the white or black boards have been replaced by digital boards, making them into "smart schools." In the past, teachers had to look back and forth into the books while using their own content to teach on primitive boards or on those boards. But we already have content stored on the digital whiteboards that can be utilised for teaching. This is how the development of smart classroom digital boards was influenced by technology, user needs, and experience.

2. Physical process- In the past, students had to wait in line before being allowed to view the notice board for the results of their 10th or 12th grade boards. Prior to that, pupils had to wait until the results were published in the daily newspaper. However, it is now quite simple for students to quickly verify their exam results online. This is where UX has played a part in the edtech business, as this process of examining boards results at their own pace and comparable other processes have undergone a drastic evolution.

Chapter-5

Approach to UX/UI Problems

A UX strategy means extensively understanding the users through research, information organization, visual design (and other methods), all with the objective of meeting user needs elegantly. It involves bringing users at the forefront of the design and development process, as well as establishing an iterative cycle of study, design, and evaluation.

The two basic beginning points for UX design projects in the industry are either an entirely new problem statement to tackle or an improvisation of the user experience of an already existing product. Therefore, let's go in-depth on a few general processes that could be followed for any UX project. This method is not linear and may alter depending on what has to be done at any given time. The steps chosen simply depend on the designer's perception of the best course of action for their project.

Here are a few steps/processes that a designer might take to finish their project, in line with their perceptions

Desk Research- Secondary research is also referred to as desk research. There are two main categories of research activities: primary research (where you move out on your own and search for things) and secondary research (where you review what other people have done). Desk research doesn't involve gathering data. Instead, as a user researcher conducting desk research, your job is to study the results of prior studies to get a thorough knowledge of the subject.

Desk research must be done as a first step as you won't be able to tell when you've found anything new if you aren't aware of what has come before. Besides that, when you speak with users and stakeholders directly, your credibility will be apparent. In the absence of this "due diligence," you risk asking stupid or pointless questions and having participants end your sessions early.

Field Research- Field observations are research activities that take place in the user's environment. They provide several insights since they are contextually appropriate. Because the individuals are monitored in their natural working environment, you will be able to eliminate many errors that would have occurred if you used any other method. Field studies will assist you in understanding the setting in which users accomplish activities, understanding their needs, collecting user tales, and so on. It will assist the researcher in understanding the user's point of view, the numerous concerns that they confront in their surroundings, problems that are beyond their control, and so on.

Ethnography- A qualitative user research method is ethnography. It is the process by which a researcher becomes involved in the culture and behaviour of the environment under study. In this situation, the researcher observes the behaviours and interactions of that particular community, and the observations are put in a document which is also called "Ethnography". It is a critical component of user research since it provides a comprehensive insight of a group's behaviour, culture, and norms. For a user experience researcher Ethnography is a versatile research method that gives first-hand information about users. Users' activities and behaviours are tracked in their natural environment. This allows the researcher to study the users in real time and uncover pain points, challenges, and edge cases that will assist in the development of solutions.

Demography- The systematic, statistical study and analysis of the population is referred to as demography. It attempts to comprehend the population's dynamics, trends, and processes by focusing on specific demographic factors such as birth, migration, ageing, and death. These mechanisms contribute to population change and demographic trends such as **the sex ratio, which is the number of females per 1000 males, and other related trends.**

Target Audience- The target audience is a specified group of people/customers who are looking to meet the needs that your product satisfies. In other words, if your firm sells a product or service that might solve a certain problem for individuals, you must identify people who would be interested in your products or services, and these people will be your target audience.

Competitive Analysis- A UX competitive analysis is an essential component of UX research. It's a chance for designers to focus on what works, avoid what doesn't, and discover gaps in order to acquire a competitive advantage. A UX competitive analysis can also help designers in better understanding their users. UX researchers can better understand what excites and frustrates customers by viewing the competition through their customers' perspective.

Heuristic Evaluation- A heuristic strategy is a method of discovery or problem solving that uses broad recommendations, or rules of thumb, rather than hard and fast rules. It is a guided analysis of an issue or study. A heuristic evaluation is a method of assessing and evaluating the usability of a website or product as it relates to UX and product design. A "usability audit" or an "expert evaluation" may also be used to describe it. One or more experts will evaluate how well a product complies with these heuristics using a set of heuristics to describe its usability.

Customer Journey- A customer journey is a series of contacts that a customer has with your company in order to fulfil a task, such as evaluating, onboarding, receiving support, or renewing a product or service. A customer journey map depicts an individual's interactions with a product or brand across time and across many channels. It enables businesses to have a deeper understanding of the customer experience, including all journey steps and interactions along the path to accomplishing their objectives. By identifying gaps between user expectations and perceptions at crucial points in the journey with corresponding departments and stakeholders.

Persona Defining- A user persona is a fictional representation of your ideal target audience. A user persona can help you better understand your clients' needs and desires, allowing you to create a more effective product or service. Its foundation should be market research, consumer interviews, and other data. It should include demographic information such as age, gender, and occupation, as well as personality traits and hobbies. User personas are essential in user experience design because they assist designers understand the needs and desires of their users. It is based on real-world user data, such as interviews and surveys, and it supports designers in designing designs that their customers would find useful and simple to use. Personas can also detect problems in a design before it is implemented.

Brainstorming- Brainstorming is a strategy used by design teams to generate ideas for tackling well-defined design problems. By asking "How Might We?" questions, teams explore a topic under controlled settings and in a free-thinking environment. They develop a diverse set of ideas and connect them to find effective solutions. It's especially popular with design teams because it allows them to expand in all directions. Despite having standards and a moderator to keep them on track, teams are free to use unconventional and lateral thinking to address any design problem. People can investigate a wide range of techniques by brainstorming—the more, the better—rather than simply examining conventional approaches and confronting the potential issue.

Technology Feasibility- The term "technological feasibility" relates to whether a certain approach to improving the product development process will be commercially viable in the model year for which a standard is being developed. It includes technical design documents, integration documentation, the completed and tested product design, and the operating model. The product is said to be technologically feasible when the Company has completed all planning, designing, coding, and testing efforts required to demonstrate that the product can be produced to match its design specifications, including functionalities, features, and technical performance requirements.

Task Flow- In UX design, task flows are used to help designers understand how users might use a product or service, as well as to identify any potential areas of confusion or frustration that may arise during the process. Task flows are typically generated as part of the user-centered design process and used to guide the design of user interfaces and interactions. Diagrams, wireframes, and other visual representations of task flows can be used to drive the design of everything from website layouts and navigation to the structure and content of mobile apps and other interactive products.

User Flow- A user may follow a variety of different paths when interacting with a product. A user flow is a written or digitally made visual representation of the numerous routes that might be taken when using an app or website. The flowchart begins with the user's initial engagement with the product, such as a homepage or onboarding screen, and ends with the final action or result, such as a purchase or account creation. Designers may evaluate and enhance the user experience and boost customer conversion rates by demonstrating this process. The biggest advantage is making your platform easier to use and ensuring that users don't waste time trying to figure out what to do next. In fact, there are frequently other paths a user might take to do the task. These potential patterns are depicted in user flows in a way that makes it simple for designers to evaluate the effectiveness of the interface they are developing.

Information Architecture- Information architecture places a strong emphasis on organising content in a permanent and efficient manner. Users should receive assistance in locating information and completing tasks. To do this, you must understand how the various components fit together to create the overall image as well as how various components interact with one another within the system. Its capability is to make information accessible and available. It also includes searching, browsing, categorising, and presenting pertinent and contextual information to help individuals understand their surroundings and find what they're seeking for both online and offline.

Wireframing- The wireframe of a user interface is a type of simple sketch. They serve as a structural depiction of the overall functional layout for programmers and website designers. It prioritizes the product's functionality over its appearance. This form of communication allows designers and programmers to get immediate input. Wireframes function as a form of website or software blueprint by visualizing the structure of the final output. It ensures alignment between clients, designers, and developers. The functionality and desired look of the finished product are made apparent by the visuals.

User Interface Designing- The term "UI design" describes the visually appealing layout of a user interface. It involves designing user interfaces, primarily for websites and mobile applications, with an eye toward aesthetics. Digital user interfaces are often the subject of UI design. An app, website, or other device's user interface is the point of computer and human interaction. This can include the device's keyboards, displays, and outside design. The style and feel of the product are the work of UI designers.

Prototype/ Interactions- The design of digital products like websites and applications that makes it easier for people to interact with them is known as interaction design. Aesthetics, motion, music, space, and many other factors that help users in achieving their objectives are sometimes included in the interaction, while other times it simply concerns the design itself.

An early development of a product that demonstrates the fundamentals of what a product will look like, what the product will do, and how the product operates is used to build the prototype of a digital product. It is the rough draught form of the product and is not intended to be the final edition. Although the prototype might not have all of the functionality that the finished product will have after being expertly made, it frequently contains aspects that show how the product will function. The prototype enables you to make changes while the product is still in concept stage and gives you a clear sense of what the final product will look like.

Usability Testing- Usability testing is a technique for assessing how simple it is to use a specific system or product. Its main objective is to rate how user-friendly websites, software programs, and other kinds of digital items, including mobile apps, are. In order for the company to improve the product in future versions, the aim is to discover any places where people have trouble utilizing it. For instance, by having consumers carry out particular tasks while being watched by researchers, the researcher then notes any instances where users had problems or had trouble finishing the job. This is especially true considering that users have a wide range of options and can rapidly switch to a different product if they're not satisfied with the one they're using. As a result, it can provide important information to experts in industries including marketing, user experience design, and digital product development.

Chapter-6

Laws of UX and Heuristics Laws

To judge how well a user interface has been created for its intended function, heuristics are a well-known and broadly acknowledged collection of UX concepts. They are known as heuristics because they serve as general principles rather than precise usability standards. Heuristic laws are criteria that were developed via a series of observations of various users and their expectations of perceiving a product as a good product. Here are the following ten UX Heuristics Laws:

1. **Visibility of System Status-** By offering relevant input quickly, the design should always keep customers informed of what's happening.

Users are better able to learn from their previous interactions and make plans for the future when they are aware of the system's present status. Trust in the goods and the brand are both increased by predictable interactions. For instance, Google Maps' location indicator lets users see where they are right now and plan their next move.

2. **Match between system and the real world-** The interface should be user-friendly. Instead of using internal jargon, use words, statements, and ideas that the user is already familiar with. Ensure that information appears in a logical and natural arrangement by following real-world conventions.

Your target users will have a significant impact on how you should design. Even terms, ideas, logos, and visuals that seem obvious to you and your coworkers may be unclear to your users. Users find it simpler to learn and recall how an interface works when the controls follow real-world norms and match desired consequences (this is known as natural mapping). This contributes to the development of an intuitive experience. For example, the presence of the colour green implies a successful or accurate activity. This is due to the fact that, outside of the screen, red and green are frequently associated with Stop and Go, or correct and incorrect, respectively.

3. **User control and freedom-** When performing actions, users commonly make mistakes. They need a clearly marked "emergency exit" to get away from the unpleasant action without having to go through a lengthy procedure. When people can simply back out

of a process or undo an activity, it fosters independence and confidence. Exits assist users in maintaining control of the system and avoiding becoming stuck or furious. The undo/redo feature is a common feature found in text editors. This example of allowing users to retract their actions is perhaps also the most typical one.

4. **Consistency and standards-** Users shouldn't have to guess whether certain expressions, circumstances, or actions are equivalent. Most of the time, people use digital products other than yours. Users' expectations are shaped by their interactions with those other products. Failure to maintain consistency could put users under more cognitive load by pushing them to pick up something new. For instance, the front of hotels is typically where the check-in desks are placed. Customers expect check-in desks to be located at the front of every hotel they stay at, whether locally or internationally, thus this consistency fits their expectations.

5. **Error prevention-** While clear error warnings are essential, the greatest solutions take care to avoid problems altogether. Error-prone situations should either be eliminated, checked for, and given a confirmation choice before users commit to an action. For instance, Microsoft provides the option to easily restore or recover a deleted file from the recycle bin if

the user accidentally destroyed one of the critical files while also deleting the unnecessary files. But you can only do that if you just erased, not shift+delete (permanently deleted).

6. **Recognition rather than recall-** Reduce the user's memory load by highlighting components, actions, and alternatives. The user should not be required to recall information from one section of the interface to the next. When using the design, information (e.g., field labels or menu items) should be visible or easily accessible. Humans have a limited capacity for short-term memory. Users' cognitive work is reduced by using interfaces that enhance recognition. Most people find it easier to recognise country capitals rather than recall them. People are more likely to properly answer the question Is Lisbon Portugal's capital? opposed to What is Portugal's capital? This is when recognition, rather than recall, comes into play.

7. **Flexibility and efficiency of use-** In order to accommodate both new and experienced users, shortcuts may speed up interaction for the expert user while remaining hidden from new users. Permit users to customize routine tasks. People can choose whichever method suits them best when using flexible processes because they can be implemented in several ways. For instance, Dribble offers shortcuts to carry out operations on their platform. The most common

shortcut is "L" for like. Both beginner and experienced users may utilize this with ease.

8. **Aesthetic and minimalist design-** Information that is unnecessary or rarely used shouldn't be present in interfaces. Each additional piece of information that is added to an interface competes with the essential pieces and reduces their relative visibility. This heuristic is about ensuring that the content and visual design are concentrated on the basics, not that you must adopt a flat design. As customers tend to find products with superior aesthetics and visuals to be more user friendly.It should make sure the interface's visual components complement the user's core goals. For instance, Airbnb has designed their homepage to have a quality device ratio. Because the search portion is designed simply and cleanly, the user can easily accomplish their main goal of choosing the location, checking in, and the number of guests.

9. **Help users recognize, diagnose, and recover from errors-** Error messages should be written in plain language (no error codes), identify the problem properly, and suggest a helpful solution. These error messages should also be visually enhanced to help users notice and recognise them. For instance, roadside wrong way signs warn vehicles that they are going the wrong way and instruct them to turn around.

10. **Help and documentation-** The ideal situation is when the system is self-explanatory. To ensure that users are able to fulfil their jobs, it could be required to offer documentation. The information in help and documentation should be centred on the user's work and be simple to search. It should be brief and include a list of specific actions that must be taken. For example, Airport information kiosks are instantly recognisable and provide quick and contextual solutions to consumers' needs.

In addition to these fundamental rules of heuristics, there are a number of other UX laws that address both usability and user perception as a whole.

Aesthetic and Usability Codependency- Users frequently associate attractive design with better usable design. People's minds respond favorably to appealing designs, which makes them think the design truly functions better. A design's aesthetic appeal might hide usability concerns and keep them from being identified during usability testing.

Doherty Threshold Principle- When a computer and its users communicate at a speed (400ms) that eliminates waiting for one another, productivity improves. In order to hold users' attention and boost productivity, it is advised to give system feedback within 400 milliseconds. Even when a procedure actually takes significantly less time, purposefully imposing a delay can boost faith in the process and enhance its perceived value.

Fitt's Law- The size and distance to a target affect how long it takes to capture it. Touch targets must to be big enough for users to select them precisely, have adequate space between them, and be positioned on an interface where they are simple to get.

Goal gradient effect- With increasing distance from a goal, a person is more likely to approach it. Users move more quickly in the direction that brings them closer to completing a job. To ensure that users are more likely to be motivated to complete the work, it is helpful to provide artificial progress toward a goal and a visible signal of progress.

Hick's Law- The more options there are and the more complicated they are, the longer it takes to decide. It was founded on the correlation between the number of choices present and a person's response time to each individual option. It makes sense that the user would take longer to choose which input to interact with the more choices there are to choose from. Users that are presented with numerous options must take their time to understand and make decisions, which results in them being assigned work they don't want to complete.

Jakob's Law- The majority of user time is spent on other websites. This indicates that visitors desire your website to operate similarly to every other website they are already familiar with. Users often project their expectations from one well-known product onto another that seems to be comparable. The idea is that by utilising current mental models, a better user experience could be developed where users can concentrate on their activities rather than learning new models.

Law of common region- When elements share a place with a clearly defined boundary, they are frequently seen as being members of the same groups. Users can quickly and simply understand the connections between parts and sections because of the common region, which creates a clear framework.

Law of Pragnaz- People will perceive and understand contradictory or complex images in their simplest form because doing so needs the least amount of cognitive work on their part. Because it keeps us from being overloaded with information, the human eye prefers to see simplicity and order in complicated shapes.

Miller's Law- Only 7 things, plus or minus 2, are typically retained in working memory by the average person. Keep in mind that each person's short-term memory ability will differ depending on their prior knowledge and environmental circumstances and to make content easier for people to process, comprehend, and remember, it should be divided into smaller sections.

Peak End Rule- Instead of considering the sum or average of all of the experience's moments, people tend to focus on how they felt during its high point and its low point. The final moments of the user journey should be addressed to, as people remember negative experiences more vividly than positive ones. These moments should be identified as the times when your product is most helpful or valuable to the end user.

Von Restorff Effect- The Von Restorff effect, commonly referred to as The Isolation Effect, states that when several comparable objects are present, it is most probable that the one that stands out will be recalled. It is necessary to make the crucial details or actions visually noticeable.

Zeigarnik Effect- Unfinished or interrupted tasks are more likely to be remembered than completed ones. Hence, a visible indicator of progress is therefore necessary to encourage users to finish tasks.

Chapter-7

Terminologies and Process

1. User and Customer - The user, as the name implies, is the person who 'uses' a product (here, considering a digital product). The customer, on the other hand, is the person who makes a purchase or avails of a service through a product (e.g. any e-commerce app).

2. Customer Experience - Customer experience involves all dimensions of a product's offering, such as advertising, packaging, characteristics of the product and service, dependability, and, of course, the level of customer service provided. E.g. When using a digital platform to access a service, the user explores the platform, filters or sorts the available products, chooses one, and purchases along with their preferred method of payment. The entire process of using the platform up until the point of payment falls under the category of "User Experience," whereas the process of finding the platform (through referrals, advertisements, etc.) and arriving there up until the point of delivery falls under "Customer Experience."

3. Persona - Personas are hypothetical users with characteristics and goals that correspond to the needs of a larger user group. A persona is often presented in a one- or two-page document that includes details on the context on which it is based as well as descriptions of behavior patterns, objectives, skills, attitudes, and background information. It makes sense to describe a person's product preferences and purchasing behaviors, for example, for an e-commerce platform. To create a persona as a realistic character, we often need to enhance a description with a little made-up personal information (for example, quotes from real users). E.g. When conducting surveys or interviews to understand the target users for an e-commerce product design (typically intended for people living in mountains), we notice that the majority of them have an average height of 5 Feet and that they experience a pain point while purchasing clothing online as they receive clothing that is designed for people who are an average height of 6 Feet tall. The fact that customers don't get the right clothes and have to get them altered after making an online purchase is one of their pain points, which we must address in the persona. Then we may create a filter option to sort the product according to their average height during the product development phase.

4. Digital and Physical/Tangible Product - Digital products are those that we can use and experience, such as any application or anything online. While tangible/physical products are those that we can touch and feel, such as a laptop, frying pan, pillow, etc. To further understand, think of physical/tangible products as hardware and digital products as software.

5. Visual Hierarchy - The visual hierarchy in any application refers to the arrangement or positioning of the design elements or any component on that interface such that the user's attention is guided to focus on each element or component in the intended importance order.

6. Primary and Secondary Audience - Primary audiences, also referred to as target audiences are individuals for whom the product is designed to meet demands that are specific to them. They play a significant role in determining the issue or problem for which the product is designed. Secondary audiences are individuals who are still considered customers but whose observations or pain issues are not the main focus of product development.

7. Qualitative/Primary/ Field Research - Field research is a research methodology that takes into account live observations. It is a qualitative research method that focuses on understanding and interpreting the social interactions of groups of people, communities, and society through observation and interaction with people in their natural reflexes.

8. Quantitative/ Secondary/ Desk Research - A type of market research that includes gathering and analyzing information that already exists and is easily accessed. Existing data is summarized and compiled to improve overall research effectiveness. Secondary research is research material that has been published in research reports and other similar documents. It gives context and scope to primary research findings by providing quick, credible background insights.

9. Iconography - Iconography is a symbolic representation that is used to represent characteristics, functionality, or content. Icons are intended to be simple, visual elements that are instantly recognized and understood.

10. Typography - Typography is the process of selecting font style and size based on the niche of the product and the experience of the target users. The font used is an essential factor in determining the impact of the product's look and feel on users.

11. Color Theory - In general, color theory refers to the use of colors in any aspect of design as per the meaning of the colors they reflect. When we think about any product, whether it be digital or physical, the colors that are incorporated in it serve a purpose that is specific to that product. For instance, the color blue indicates a sense of trust, and blue is the color that most hospitals use. So this is how the color theory is applied to various items following the message that the brand wants to convey to its target audience.

12. **Use Case Scenario** - When we are in the middle of developing a product (from the ground up, research to market launch), we have a diverse set of users with varying approaches and perspectives on how to use that product. This introduces the use case scenario, in which the user takes multiple paths to reach the goal, each of which is considered a use case scenario.

13. **Brainstorming** - Brainstorming is a problem-solving method used in groups that involve the momentary contribution of creative ideas and solutions. This technique necessitates a lengthy, free-flowing discussion in which each member of the group is encouraged to think aloud and propose as many ideas as possible based on their diverse knowledge. It is a method for developing new concepts to solve problems by looking at them in a new direction. Some of these ideas can be developed into unique, creative solutions to problems, while others can initiate new ones.

14. **Task Flow** - Task flows are typically linear, displaying the high-level steps a person would take to

achieve a specific goal. They are all sequential, with no options or decision points.

15. **User Flow** - User flows often show how a particular person might navigate the design. However, unlike task flows, user flows feature choice points at which the persona's path to the desired goal can vary depending on the decisions the persona must make when interacting with the design. A set or series of task flows can be embedded within user flows.

16. **Gamification** - The technique of incorporating interactive elements into your user experience and encouraging people to interact with your resource in a game-like way is known as gamification. It's a great strategy to draw in your target market and boost user interaction with your app or website. Users desire to have a specific objective to work toward, even if the reward is not tangible.

17. **Pain Points** - A customer's "pain point" is a very specific issue they are having with your brand of product or service. When a consumer is using an e-commerce platform, for instance, and the checkout and payment procedure takes a long time, they can just give up and switch to another e-commerce supplier. A product team's ability to recognize and address this client's pain point helps increase conversion rates.

18. **Conversion Rate** - The percentage of users who perform the intended action is known as the conversion

rate. For example, the number of website visitors who make a purchase there serves as the ideal example of conversion rate.

19. User Research - User experience (UX) research is the methodical study of target users and their needs with the goal of providing design processes with relevant contexts and insights. UX researchers use a variety of techniques to identify issues and design opportunities. By doing this, they make important discoveries that can be used to inform the design process. We can provide people with the finest solutions when we conduct UX research since we can identify their unique needs.

20. UI Elements - The components we need to create apps or websites are known as user interface (UI) elements. They enhance a user interface's interactivity by acting as touchpoints for the user as they move around; consider buttons, scrollbars, menu items, checkboxes, etc.

As part of creating a visual language and ensuring consistency throughout a product, several aspects are employed to build the user interface, making it intuitive and simple for users to use without spending too much thought.

21. User-Centric Design - The user is taken into account first when designing, and solutions are chosen accordingly. Instead of making the user attempt to understand a product, the usability of a user-centric product is created following user expectations and industry best practices.

22. System-Centric Design - The goal of the system-centric design method is to organize the system's functions and construct the final product using the designer's interpretation and application of systems thinking. The requirements and functionality of the product are taken into account first in this method. For instance, if a business wants a specific set of features to be a product and then invests time in teaching its staff how to operate that product. These products follow up with system specifications as opposed to user needs and industry best practices.

23. Information Architecture - The goal of information architecture (IA) is to organize, structure, and classify content in a practical and long-lasting manner. Users are supposed to be assisted in finding information and finishing tasks. To accomplish this, we must recognize how the different components are arranged together according to the mental mode to form the bigger picture and how components interact with one another in the system.

24. Wireframe - A website or an application service can be designed structurally using wireframes. In order to lay out content and functionality on a page, while taking into account user needs and user journeys, a wireframe is frequently used. Before adding visual design and content to a page, the basic framework of the page is established using wireframes early in the development process. This is the basic structure of the finished product, which comes in three varieties: Low, Medium, and High Fidelity.

25. **Prototype** - A prototype or imitation of the finished product that UX teams test ahead of time. Before sharing concepts with stakeholders and ultimately handing off the final designs to engineering teams for the development process, a prototype aims to test and validate ideas. Prototypes, which usually lack coding, are exact replicas of how a finished product will look. The majority of the final UI design and user interaction that the end product will have is incorporated into them.

26. **Problem Statement** - A problem statement is a brief explanation of a problem that needs to be solved or a situation that needs to be improved. It pinpoints the difference between the desired (goal) state and the present (problem) condition of a process or product. Three things are commonly included in problem statements: the problem itself, which should be stated concisely and with enough background information to explain why it is significant; the solution to the problem, which is frequently viewed as a claim or a

working thesis; and the goal and the statement of objectives.

27. Customer Journey - The entire set of the interactions that customers have with your business, brand, or product is known as the customer journey. The customer journey captures the entire experience of being a customer, and not just focusing on a single event or interaction. It covers every touchpoint the customer must have experienced in order to provide us a clue about which touchpoints to investigate further and which observations to record for incorporation into building of the business, brand, or product.

28. Usability - Usability testing is a technique used by designers, user researchers, and usability professionals to evaluate a product's usability. This procedure could reveal a user's expectations, preferences, and issues. They can improve a design after they have a better understanding of what is working and what isn't. When a product has good usability, customers may do their tasks quickly, with little effort and error, and ultimately feel satisfied. This becomes crucial for product manufacturers to draw in buyers. Better usability attracts customers and increases the likelihood that they will suggest that brand to others.

29. Mental Model - A mental model is an explanation of one's thoughts about how something works in the real world. It is a mental image of the environment, including the relationships between its numerous aspects, as well as a person's intuitive grasp of their own actions and the consequences.

30. Omni present Vs Omni channel - If an app or a digital product is available across various platforms or devices, such as mobile, television, desktop, tablet, and so on, the product's ecosystem is said to be Omnipresent. Whereas Omni channel occurs when a person commences a task in an app and then continues that task on any other device from which they log in again.

31. Ethnography - Ethnography is the study of people's natural and most real behaviors in their real world. In UX design, ethnography is used as a study method to explore how people engage with technology in their natural, real-world surroundings.

32. Demography - The systematic, statistical study and analysis of the population is referred to as demography. It attempts to understand the population's behaviors, trends, and processes by focusing on specific demographic phenomena such as birth, migration, ageing, and death. Demographic data in UX research aids in understanding the patterns of target users, which improves in the development of a user-friendly product.

33. Best Practices - Best practices in User Experience provide the framework for a repeatable process, allowing us to provide the benefit of user experience in a reasonable length of time while avoiding the mistakes made by others who came before us. They allow teams to execute with certainty that they are doing the right thing in the right order. In any e-commerce app, for example, we often observe the payment process once the user has confirmed their order and address. This is currently considered best practice. So, even if a new e-commerce app enters the market, it will follow the same flow because it is the best practice and where people expect such flow to appear.

34. **MVP or Minimum Viable Produc**t - By first developing a minimum viable product (MVP), you can detect friction spots, correct faults, and minimize unnecessary problems as you progress through the process. The concept of an MVP is straightforward: it is a basic, a prototype version of what you imagine as your ultimate product, with only a limited set of core features. Before launching your final product, you can utilize your MVP to collect new data and test assumptions.

35. **Responsive Design** - Responsive design is a web design method in which the interface adapts to the device's layout, allowing for usability, navigation, and decision making. To maintain content uniformity across devices, media queries allow the design to automatically convert to browser space, and design elements are sized in relative units (%).

36. Style Guide - UI style guides are a comprehensive set of design rules for UI elements and interactions used in various web/app products that ensure product consistency among design teams, companies, and brands. It contains all of the UI rules, such as component and font sizes, component statuses, and so forth.

37. Laws of UX - The UX Laws are a set of best practices that designers can utilize when developing user interfaces. Heuristic Laws, User Experience Principles, Gestalt's Laws, and Cognitive Biases are examples of these.

38. Feasibility - The feasibility of any feature of a product refers to its ability to be developed utilising the technologies that are accessible from a development standpoint.

39. Ideation - Ideation is the practice of generating a huge number of ideas about a particular topic without attempting to judge or evaluate them. While the ultimate goal of ideation is to produce a high-quality design that solves a specific problem, the emphasis is on number rather than quality. Ideation is only one step in the whole UX design process; after ideas are generated, they must be analyzed individually to choose which ideas (or sections of ideas) to pursue. The greater the number, the better the ideations.

9 789356 685338